5 34 deP

Pinna, Simon, de
AUTHOR

Sound
TITLE

Science Projects

DATE DUE	BORROWER'S NAME	ROOM NUMBER

SOUND

Simon de Pinna
Photography by Chris Fairclough

RSVP
RAINTREE
STECK-VAUGHN
PUBLISHERS
The Steck-Vaughn Company

Austin, Texas

Published by Raintree Steck-Vaughn Publishers, an imprint of Steck-Vaughn Company

Library of Congress Cataloging-in-Publication Data
de Pinna, Simon.
Sound / Simon de Pinna.
    p.   cm.—(Science Projects)
    Includes bibliographical references and index.
    Summary: Introduces the concept of sound and its properties through brief explanations followed by simple science experiments.
    ISBN 0-8172-4944-3
    1. Sound—Experiments—Juvenile literature.
    2. Science projects—Juvenile literature.
    [1. Sound—Experiments. 2. Experiments.]
    I. Title. II. Series: Science projects.
    QC225.5.P53   1998
    534'.078—dc21   97-5989

Printed in Italy. Bound in the United States.
1 2 3 4 5 6 7 8 9 0 02 01 00 99 98

Picture acknowledgments
The publishers would like to thank the following for permission to reproduce their pictures:

Bruce Coleman: pages 4 (Jonathan T. Wright), 14 (Kim Taylor), 22 (Werner Layer), 38 (Kevin Burchett); **Images Colour Library:** pages 8, 24; **Redferns:** page 20 (David Redfern); **Science Photo Library:** pages 26 top (Yves Baulieu), 26 bottom (Mehau Kulyk), 41 (Damien Lovegrove), 42 (James King-Holmes); **Tony Stone Images:** pages 17 (Kindra Clineff), 34 (Everett Johnson), 36 (Bruno De Hogues); **Vodafone Group:** page 42; **Zefa:** page 33 (L. Villota), cover (H. J. Dorf)

Illustrations: Julian Baker, p. 20: Kieran Walsh, p. 27: Colin Newman
Commissioned photography: Chris Fairclough

CONTENTS

SOUND MESSAGES

Sounds play an important part in our lives. They carry a great deal of information about the objects that make the sounds and the material through which the sounds travel.

There are a wide variety of sounds in our environment, ranging from birdsong and leaves rustling in the wind to the sound of a car's engine, the telephone, and jet aircraft. There are many sounds that we enjoy hearing or making ourselves, for example, listening to birds or playing a musical instrument. But not all the sounds we hear are pleasing to the ear. Some sounds can be unpleasant—we call those noise.

How many sources of sound can you identify in this crowded street in Bombay?

A SOUND ALPHABET

MATERIALS
- a cassette recorder with a microphone
- a blank cassette

1. Create a cassette of sounds to give to a younger child who is learning the alphabet. Record yourself saying "A is for..." and then record a sound linked with the object beginning with the letter A. Some examples could include someone biting into an apple, the sound of an ax chopping wood, or an airplane flying overhead. You may need to give an extra clue, depending on the age and experience of the child listening to the cassette.

2. Do this for all the alphabet letters. Don't leave out any letters even if you can't find objects for them or cannot record a sound for them. Either make the sound of the object yourself, or give a different clue.

SOUND DETECTIVE

Record sounds from different parts of your school, including the gym and on the playing fields outside. Make recordings around where you live, in the street and in the stores. Make sure you ask the owner's permission before you start recording in a store. Then play the tape for your friends and see if they can guess where the recordings were made. How many different sounds can your friends identify? Can they distinguish any noises not made by humans?

MATERIALS

- a cassette recorder with a microphone
- a blank cassette

DID YOU KNOW?

The mating calls of male frogs send out several messages to the females. Their calls help identify the species and the size of the male. Unfortunately for the frog they can also identify its position to a predator such as a frog-eating bat!

GOOD VIBRATIONS

You hear a sound when a moving object makes the air vibrate. These vibrations travel through the air in the form of waves. High-pitched sounds, such as the sound of a whistle, create waves that are close together. Lower-pitched sounds, like thunder, rumble, and the sound waves are farther apart.

The pitch, or note, of a sound is determined by its frequency. Frequency is the number of waves that pass a point in one second and is measured in hertz (Hz). Most of us can hear sounds with a frequency as low as 20 Hz, and a high-pitched scream could have a frequency of up to 10,000 Hz.

SOUND WAVES

The distance between the tops of two waves is called the sound's wavelength. The higher the frequency of the note, the closer the waves and the shorter their wavelength. Low notes have a long wavelength. There are about 55 ft. (17 m) between the waves of a 20-Hz note, but less than 1.5 in. (4 cm) between the wave-tops of a 10,000-Hz note. If one sound is louder than another, its waves will be higher than the quieter sound, even if it has the same frequency and wavelength. The height of a sound wave is called its amplitude.

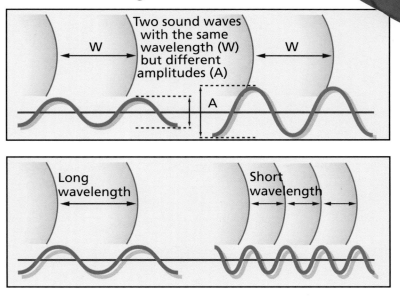

Two sound waves with the same wavelength (W) but different amplitudes (A)

W   W   A

Long wavelength   Short wavelength

A WAVE MACHINE

1. Cut a piece out of the balloon that will fit over one end of the cardboard tube, with a .75 in. to 1 in. (2 to 3 cm) overlap.

2. Wrap the elastic band over the end of the tube so that it grips the sheet of balloon tightly. Then stick the square of kitchen foil onto the center of the stretched balloon.

3. In a dimly lit room, hold the tube up to your mouth. Get a friend to stand a little in front and to the left-hand side of you, and aim the flashlight at the foil so that the beam bounces off it.

4. Get another friend to stand a similar distance away and on the right-hand side of you. That friend should hold the sheet of paper so that it acts like a screen, and you can see a bright area of light reflected off the foil.

5. Keeping the tube, flashlight, and screen steady, shout into the open end of the tube, and see how the sound affects the spot of light on the screen. The balloon acts like a drum skin, moving in and out with the sound waves.

6. Watch the vibrations of the spot of light on the screen. Can you see the spot jump about as the piece of balloon vibrates? What is the effect of making louder and softer sounds, or higher and lower notes, on the number and size of the vibrations?

MATERIALS

- a cardboard tube at least 2 in. (6 cm) in diameter and 12 in. (30 cm) long
- a balloon
- an elastic band to fit tightly around the end of the tube
- a flashlight
- scissors and glue
- a piece of smooth kitchen foil, 1 in. (3 cm) square
- a sheet of white paper

MAKING WAVES

Both sound and light travel as waves, but sound waves behave in a different way than light waves. Light waves can move either up and down or from side to side. They are called transverse waves. The waves you see on water are also transverse waves.

Sound travels in waves just as waves travel across the surface of water. However, sound waves are longitudinal, whereas water waves are transverse. Light waves are also transverse.

ROPES AND SPRINGS

1. Tie one end of the length of rope around a post or door handle, and hold the other end fairly tight.

2. Shake your hand up and down to make a wave in the rope. This is a transverse wave, like a water wave or a light wave.

3. Shake your hand faster. What happens to the number of waves? What happens to the waves when you shake your hand farther from side to side or up and down?

MATERIALS
- a long length of thin rope
- a Slinky® made up of many coils

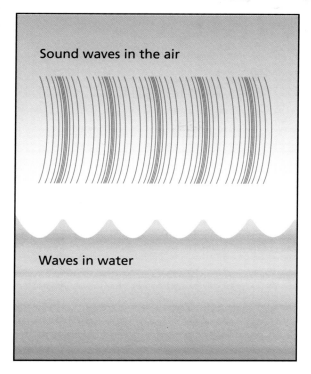

Sound waves in the air

Waves in water

Water waves (bottom) are transverse. They move up and down as they travel. Sound waves (top) are longitudinal. They travel as ripples of squeezed air.

Sound waves move back and forth in the direction that the sound is traveling. They are called longitudinal waves. If you watch the thin cone on the front of a loudspeaker you can see that the sounds make it bounce in and out. When the cone vibrates, it pushes and pulls the air in front of it, first squeezing the air as it pushes it and then stretching the air as the cone pulls back. If you put your hand in front of a working loudspeaker you can feel the air vibrating.

When something causes an object to vibrate, the sound waves spread out as ripples of squeezed air in the same way that ripples of water spread out. The number of these high pressure waves per second is the frequency of the sound. The amount that the air is squeezed in each ripple is the amplitude of the sound. The greater the squeeze, the louder the sound.

4. Stretch out the Slinky® on a smooth floor, and ask a friend to hold one end.

5. Holding the other end, give it a sharp push toward your friend. Notice the wave of tight coils move along the Slinky®. This is a longitudinal wave, like a sound wave.

What should you do to make waves in the Slinky® of higher frequency and greater amplitude?

DID YOU KNOW?

During a storm in November 1940, gusts of wind made the Tacoma Narrows Bridge in Washington State vibrate in such a way that a wave built up along the bridge. The bridge twisted back and forth so violently that it shook itself to pieces.

SOUND CARRIERS

Sound can travel through any substance, whether it is a solid, a liquid, or a gas, but the speed at which sound waves travel is different in each substance.

Substances are made up of particles. The particles in a solid object are packed closely together and, therefore, can only vibrate back and forth a very small distance. When an object vibrates against a solid substance, such as a wall, the vibrations are passed on from one particle to its neighbor, like people jostling one another in a crowd. The extra energy created by the jostling particles is the sound wave traveling through the solid object. Sound waves travel very quickly through solids.

In a liquid, the particles are much farther apart than in a solid and can move in all directions. Some of the energy passed on from the vibrating object to the particles in a liquid is changed into movement energy. This makes the particles move faster, and less energy is passed on to other particles as a sound wave. Sound travels more slowly in liquids than in solids.

The particles in a gas are farthest apart of all and travel at high speed. When an object vibrates in a gas, such as air, a lot of the energy is used to make the air particles move faster. Because they are so far apart, very little of the energy is passed on from particle to particle as a sound wave. Sound travels slowest of all in gases.

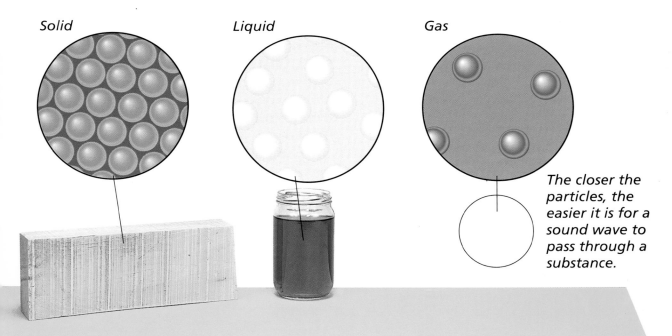

Solid

Liquid

Gas

The closer the particles, the easier it is for a sound wave to pass through a substance.

FEEL THE SOUND

1. Stand 6 ft. (2 m) away from a friend so he or she can see only one of your ears. Put your hand over your other ear.

MATERIALS

- an alarm clock with a bell
- a nail
- a 6-ft. (2-m) measuring tape

2. Ask your friend to hold the head of the nail against the bell of the alarm clock, and then set off the alarm clock for a few seconds. Listen carefully to the sound.

3. Try the test again with your ear pressed against a wall and with your other ear covered as before. This time, your friend should hold the nail between the bell of the alarm clock and the wall so that it is touching both of them.

4. Listen to the sound of the alarm. Which is louder—the sound in air or the sound in the wall?

5. Repeat the experiment with your ear against other surfaces, such as a table, a metal radiator, a plastic pipe, or the floor. For an accurate test, make sure you are 6 ft. (2 m) away from the alarm clock each time.

Which substance made the sound seem loudest? That substance carries the sound best. It is a good conductor of sound.

DID YOU KNOW?

You cannot hear an explosion in space. Sound waves can only travel when there are particles to pass on the energy. There are hardly any particles in space—it is a vacuum—so nothing can make a sound.

SPEED OF SOUND

If you watch a sprint race, you will see smoke from the starter's pistol a fraction of a second before you hear the bang. The sound waves made by the pistol reach your ears a short time after the light from the smoke reaches your eyes. This happens because light travels nearly one million times faster than sound—186,000 mi. per second compared with 1,100 ft. per second.

This explains why you often see lightning flash a short time before you hear the clap of thunder. If you see lightning flash, count the time in seconds until you hear the thunder. For every 5 seconds, the thunder travels 1 mi., so you can tell whether the storm is moving toward you or away from you by comparing the times for several claps.

SOUND BARRIER

Slower than the speed of sound

At the speed of sound

Faster than the speed of sound

We speak of an aircraft "breaking the sound barrier" when the speed at which it travels surpasses the speed of sound. As an aircraft in flight reaches the speed of sound, which is about 750 mi. per hour, the sound waves pile up in front of it. This is called the shock wave. If the aircraft flies even faster, it breaks through the shock wave, and a sonic boom, just like a clap of thunder, is heard on the ground. There can even be enough energy in a sonic boom to shatter windows where the shock wave reaches the ground.

SOUND VERSUS LIGHT

MATERIALS
- 3 colored balls
- 3 whistles
- a stopwatch

1. Three experimenters stand as far apart as possible on a playing field or large open space. Each person has a colored ball and a whistle. A fourth person is the observer and stands next to one of the experimenters.

2. At a signal from the observer, experimenter 1 drops a ball, and the observer starts the stopwatch.

3. Experimenter 2 drops a ball when he or she sees the first ball fall. Experimenter 3 does the same when he or she sees experimenter 2's ball fall. The observer stops the watch when he or she sees experimenter 3 drop the ball. The observer should make a note of the time taken.

DID YOU KNOW?

The speed of an aircraft compared with the speed of sound is called the Mach number. This is named after an Austrian scientist, Ernst Mach. Concorde, the fastest passenger aircraft, flies at Mach 2—twice the speed of sound. The fastest military jets can fly at more than Mach 3.

4. Repeat the experiment, but instead of dropping a ball, each experimenter blows a whistle when he or she hears the whistle of the previous experimenter. The observer notes the time it takes between the sound of the first and the third whistle.

Compare the results of steps 2 and 3 with those of step 4, as recorded by the observer. What difference do you notice between the time it takes for the sound of the whistle to go around the triangle of experimenters compared to the light signal from the colored balls?

HIGHER AND LOWER

You may have noticed that when a fast-moving police car or emergency vehicle comes toward you, the pitch of the sound from its siren seems to rise slightly and then drop as it moves away. This change in sound is even easier to hear when a jet aircraft flies over you—the faster the source of a sound, the greater the rise in frequency as the sound maker approaches you and the greater the fall in frequency as it goes away.

As a police siren moves closer, the sound waves are squeezed, creating a higher-pitched sound. As it moves away again, the sound has a lower note.

Wavelength longer and frequency lower

Wavelength shorter and frequency higher

Siren

Direction of motion

Bats use the Doppler effect to calculate the position and speed of a flying insect by sending out high-frequency sound waves.

This effect was first noticed by the Austrian scientist Christian Doppler in 1842, but with light rather than sound waves. He noticed that the color changed in distant stars as they moved away. Doppler's principle shows that when a source of sound with a certain frequency comes toward you, the sound waves bunch up as the source catches up with them. More of the sound waves arrive at your ears each second than if the source was not moving, so the frequency of the sound you hear is higher. As the source of the sound goes away from you, the sound waves are farther apart than if the source was still, which means that the frequency of the sound seems lower.

DOPPLER TUBES

1. Tie a short cardboard tube to a 3-ft.-(1–m) length of string or thread.

2. Twirl the tube above your head. Stand clear of people and buildings and notice how the pitch of the sound changes. How does changing the size of the tube affect the note that it makes as it moves away from and toward you? How does changing the speed you twirl the tube affect the note that it makes as it moves away from and toward you?

3. Tie a whistle on to the string and see how the speed you twirl the string affects the frequency of the sound the whistle makes.

MATERIALS

- thin string
- cardboard tubes of various sizes (no more than 8 in. [20 cm] long)
- a whistle

DID YOU KNOW?

Many burglar alarms use the Doppler effect. A room can be filled with invisible infrared waves transmitted from an electronic device in one corner. If the waves are reflected back to the device, it can sense when someone or something is moving and sound an alarm.

THE HUMAN VOICE

There are two pairs of vocal cords in the human larynx. One pair, the false vocal cords, helps close the opening to your windpipe when you swallow, so that food doesn't go "down the wrong way" when you are eating. Below the false cords are the true vocal cords. They are attached at both ends to blocks of cartilage at the front and back of the larynx. When you breathe in and out, the vocal cords open and air passes easily between them. But when you want to speak or sing, the vocal cords come closer together. Vibration of the cords by air coming out of the lungs produces sounds that are made louder, or amplified, by the hollow shape of the voice box.

The vocal cords change in size and shape as a child grows up. As a boy becomes a man, his larynx becomes larger and his vocal cords slacken, producing a deeper voice. This does not happen in girls. A girl's larynx, unlike a boy's, does not grow larger as she grows up. This means that a woman's voice is not very different from a girl's voice.

VOCAL CORDS

You make sounds by forcing air out of your lungs so that it passes between vibrating bands of flexible tissue at the top of your windpipe. These bands are called the vocal cords, and they are inside a space in your throat known as the larynx, or voice box.

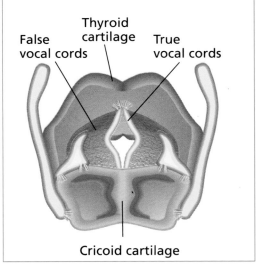

False vocal cords

Thyroid cartilage

True vocal cords

Cricoid cartilage

SOUND EFFECTS

1. Write a script or a scene from a short story about one or more of the following topics: a jungle expedition; going shopping in town; visiting a zoo or a music store.

MATERIALS
● a notebook and pen

2. Include as many descriptions of things that make sounds as you can. On your own or with a friend, act out your story as though you were performing it on the radio. You should make as many of the sound effects as possible with your voices. How many can you make? Which are the most difficult sounds to copy?

You control the sounds to make words by changing the position of the vocal cords as well as other body parts, including the tongue, lips, teeth, and jaw.

RHYMING SOUNDS

MATERIALS
- a book of verse or short poems

1. Rhyming sounds are groups of different letters that sound the same or similar, even if they are spelled differently, such as kite and fight or eight and late. Find a favorite poem, or write one yourself, that makes uses of rhymes. Read it out loud to hear how well the sounds rhyme.

2. Try reading the poem in a different accent from your normal speech. Accents are the varied ways in which people from different regions or countries with the same language speak. What do you have to do with your vocal cords, mouth, and even the way you breathe in order to speak with a different accent?

HEARING SOUNDS

The ear is one of the sense organs of the body. The ears change sound waves into electrical signals, which are a form of energy your brain can understand. How do they do that?

There are three main parts to the ear: the outer ear, the middle ear, and the inner ear. The outer ear includes the ear flap, or pinna, which funnels sound waves down the ear canal to a thin sheet of stretched skin, called the eardrum.

The eardrum is the first part of the middle ear. Attached to the back of it, well inside your skull, are a chain of three tiny bones called the hammer, anvil, and stirrup. Vibrations passing down the ear canal make the eardrum vibrate, and this starts the bones moving back and forth. The way that the bones

are joined means that the sound waves are amplified as they cross the middle ear. So that the eardrum can vibrate freely, the middle ear is filled with air, which is carried from the back of the mouth by the Eustachian tube.

The inner ear contains two parts: a bony tube called the cochlea, which looks like a snail shell, and a set of three bony hoops called the semicircular canals. Both parts are filled with a fluid. When vibrations of the stirrup bone reach the cochlea, they enter the fluid by vibrating a sheet of skin, the oval window, stretched across a hole in the cochlea. Inside the cochlea are special cells that respond to vibrations by sending out small electrical signals along a nerve to the brain, which interprets them as sounds.

THE HUMAN EAR

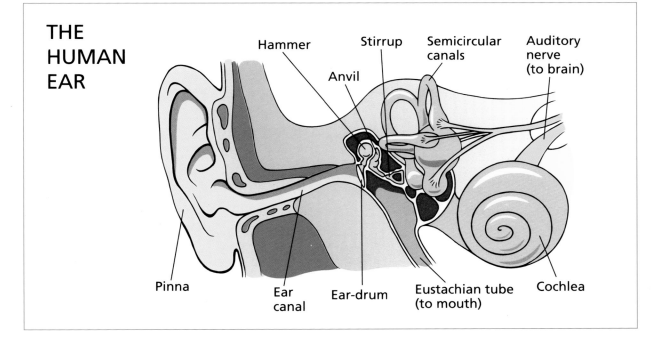

Labels: Hammer, Anvil, Stirrup, Semicircular canals, Auditory nerve (to brain), Pinna, Ear canal, Ear-drum, Eustachian tube (to mouth), Cochlea

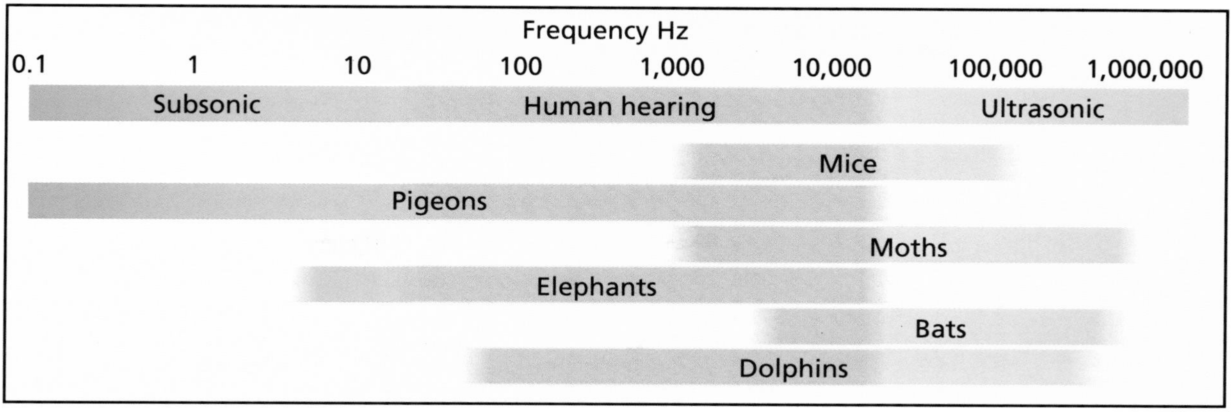
Frequency Hz
0.1
1
10
100
1,000
10,000
100,000
1,000,000
Subsonic
Human hearing
Ultrasonic
Mice
Pigeons
Moths
Elephants
Bats
Dolphins

This diagram shows the range of frequencies heard by different animals.

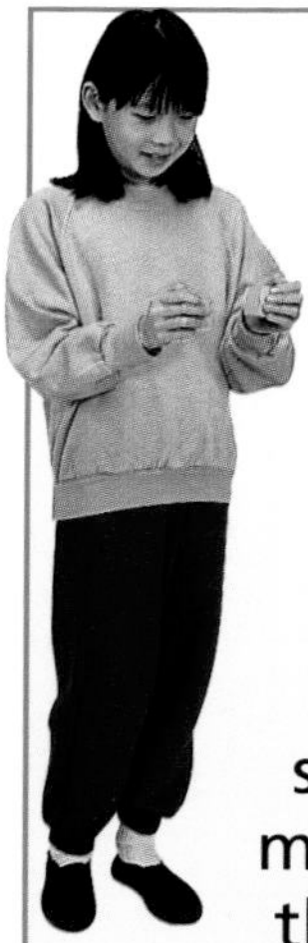

WHICH DIRECTION?

MATERIALS

- 3 or 4 pairs of wooden blocks
- a blindfold
- a pen and paper
- sound-absorbing materials, such as cotton and foam rubber

1. In a large space, stand inside a circle of three or four friends and ask one of them to blindfold you. Another friend should act as observer and record the results.

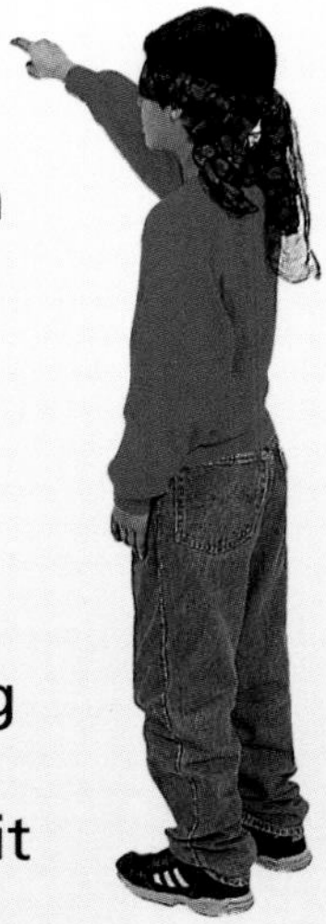

2. Each friend should take turns making a sound with the blocks, but not in any fixed order around the circle. The friends should all make the same sound each time.

3. As soon as the sound is made, and without turning around, you must point to where you think it was made. The observer decides if you are correct and puts a check mark on your hearing record.

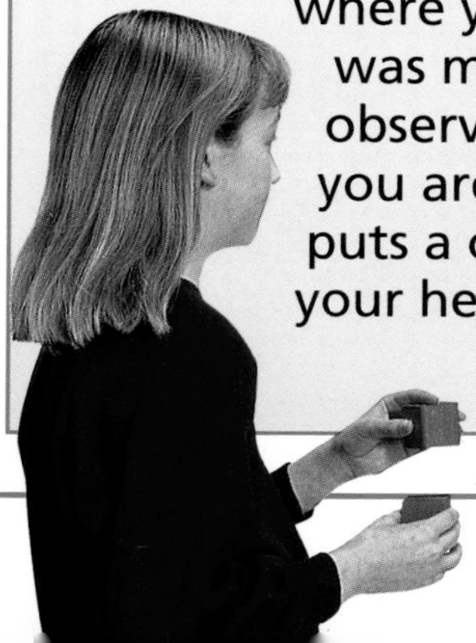

4. Keep doing this until your hearing in all directions has been tested. Where was it easiest to locate the direction of the sounds?

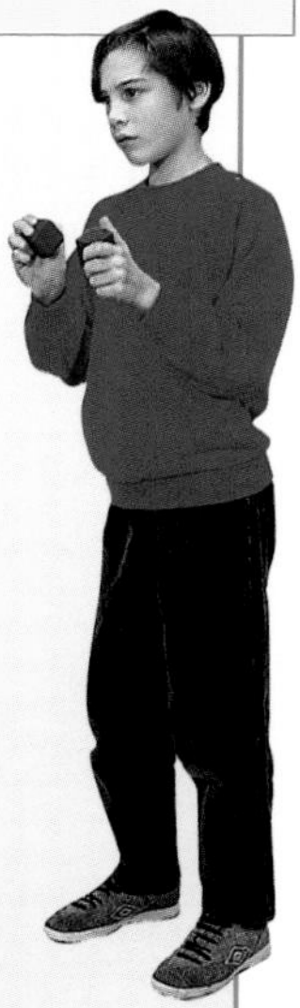

5. Try the experiment again, but with one ear covered with soundproofing material. What effect does that have? Why is it important to be able to hear a sound with both ears?

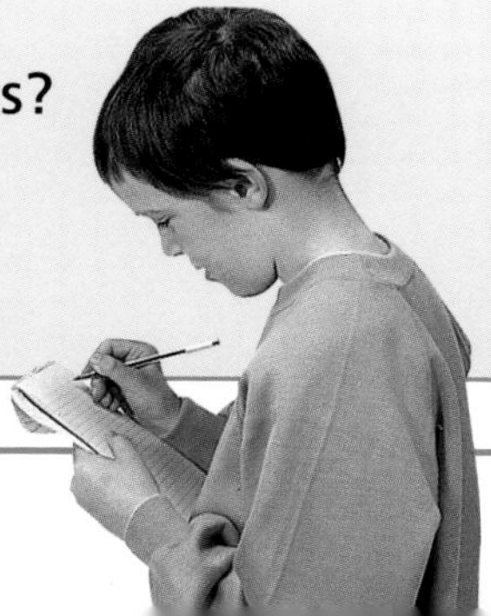

DEAFNESS

Deafness is a loss of hearing. It can be partial or total, and temporary or permanent, depending on the cause. Anything that keeps vibrations from passing through the eardrum into the cochlea or prevents the cochlea from sending nerve messages to the brain will make you deaf.

Evelyn Glennie is a percussionist who has achieved worldwide fame and success despite her impaired hearing. Some of the world's most famous composers and musicians have suffered from hearing impairment.

SIGN LANGUAGE

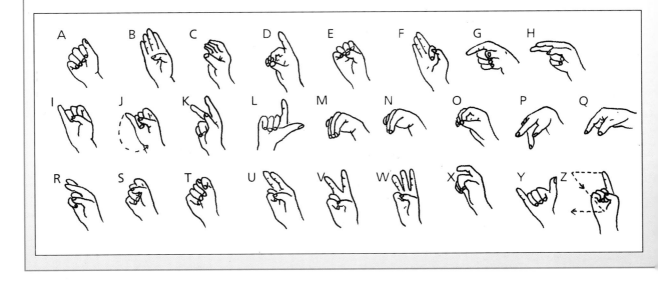

A common cause of temporary deafness is a buildup of wax in the outer ear. The wax is important for trapping dust and bacteria, but sometimes a thick layer of wax keeps the eardrum from vibrating properly. Full hearing comes back when the wax is dissolved and removed.

The eardrum itself can be damaged by very loud sounds, such as a severe bump on the head or a sudden change in air pressure. Any of these things can make a hole in the eardrum, and, although the eardrum can sometimes heal itself, deafness can be permanent.

Infections in the ear may damage the eardrum or the small bones in the middle ear. If these become jammed together, they cannot carry vibrations to the cochlea, and the person may become partially or totally deaf. A hearing aid can often help in these cases. A hearing aid contains a microphone that amplifies certain sound frequencies. Infections can also damage the cochlea or the auditory nerve. In those cases, a hearing aid is of little use, and a surgeon may fit a cochlea implant instead. This is a battery-powered device that converts sounds into electrical signals and passes them directly to the auditory nerve. Although it does not give back the same hearing that the deaf person may have had before, with training it gives a sensation of sound.

Hearing impaired people can "talk" to other people by using sign language.

DID YOU KNOW?

Many deaf people use hearing aids to amplify the sounds around them. Unfortunately, the aids also amplify unwanted noise and background sounds. Many public buildings now have induction loops fitted when they are built. These are coils of wire around a room that transmit frequencies in a range that people can hear by means of a magnetic field. Anyone using a hearing aid should adjust it to receive the transmissions when they are inside the induction loop.

---

1. The diagrams opposite illustrate the finger shapes that mean the letters of the alphabet. You will need to refer to this diagram frequently.

2. Can you find the letters that make up your name? Practice signing your name to a friend.

3. Make up a short message and sign it to a friend. Can your friend understand it by looking at the signs shown here?

TURN UP THE VOLUME

You have found out that sound waves travel outward from the point where they are made, just like ripples made by a stone dropped into water. As the waves travel farther from the source, the energy spreads out and the sound becomes quieter. If you want to hear the sound louder, you need to collect more of the energy in the waves. People calling out over a long distance cup their hands in front of their mouths to make a funnel for the sound waves. In the same way, the person they are calling to will cup his or her hands behind the ears and bend them forward to catch as much of each sound wave as possible. This idea has led to inventions such as the ear trumpet and the stethoscope. These devices amplify sounds by concentrating the waves into a small space.

In addition to collecting more of the energy in the sound waves to make sounds seem louder, you can also put more energy into the waves at the source. This will increase their amplitude,

The ears of the desert fox are so large that it can hear a single grasshopper 65 ft. (20 m) away.

so the sound waves will be higher. To do this, you amplify the sound signals.

The scale for measuring loudness of sound is the decibel (dB) scale. Quiet sounds, such as breathing, are about 10 dB, whereas normal talking is about 50 dB. A jet taking off is in the range of 120 to 140 dB. Sounds at this scale can be painful to hear and are very likely to damage your hearing.

MAKING A MEGAPHONE AND AN EAR TRUMPET

1. Roll the sheets of cardboard into cone shapes. The narrow end of the megaphone should fit over your mouth. The narrow end of the ear trumpet should fit close to your ear.

MATERIALS

- 2 sheets of thin cardboard
- scissors
- tape

Loudness (dB)   Sound

Loudness (dB)

Pain threshold

140
130
120
110
100
90
80
70
60
50
40
30
20
10

The loudness of some everyday sounds measured in dB

MAKING A STETHOSCOPE

1. Push the narrow ends of two funnels into the open ends of the plastic tubing. If the tubing is too narrow, ask an adult to warm the ends near a source of heat to soften the plastic.

MATERIALS
- 20 in. (50 cm) of flexible plastic tubing
- 2 plastic funnels

2. Ask a friend to hold one of the funnels over his or her chest. Place the other funnel over your ear and listen carefully. Can you hear your friend's heart beating? Try listening for stomach rumbling sounds as well!

2. Tape the cardboard sheets so that they do not unroll. Trim the edges to make the ends even.

3. Take the ear trumpet and walk away from a friend until you can barely hear each other when talking normally. Test the megaphone and the ear trumpet by talking normally. How much farther away can you hear your friend than before?

STOP THAT NOISE!

Pollution is anything that harms or disturbs the natural environment. Just as chemicals in a river or litter in the park are pollution, unwanted noise can cause pollution. Some people cause noise pollution by playing their radios loudly, but the main problems in many areas are aircraft and traffic noise. In science, a noise is a mixture of vibrations without any smooth, regular pattern. The sound of an electric drill or a radio tuning from one station to another are examples.

Noise can be reduced by soundproofing. You have probably noticed the difference between the sound in an empty room and a furnished one. Some materials are very effective at soaking up sounds. They are often made up of fibers or foam, because these trap layers or bubbles of air. Sounds do not travel well through air. Most of the curtains, carpets, and upholstery in your home are good sound absorbers and will keep sound from traveling through windows, walls, and floors.

A lot of noise pollution can be avoided if a machine is properly designed. Modern cars contain different materials to reduce the amount of noise coming from the engine and other moving parts, as well as noise produced by the car as it moves through the air. Look around next time you are in a car. What soundproofing can you see? By replacing metal parts in cars and other machines with parts made of plastics and foams, there is now far less noise than there used to be.

Prolonged exposure to very loud noise can seriously damage the ears. That is why the forester using the chainsaw shown here is wearing ear protectors.

SOUND INSULATORS

1. Place the alarm clock on a table and set it off. Listen to the sound from across the room.

2. Take two pieces of one of the materials. Place one under the clock, and tape together two of the edges of the other piece to make a cylinder that will fit over the clock.

3. Set off the alarm and listen to the sound from across the room as before. Is the sound louder, quieter, or no different?

DID YOU KNOW?

It is possible to remove the noise from a machine by using something called antinoise. In hospitals, some body scanners have antinoise devices. These detect the noise from the scanner's working parts and feed them into a computer. The computer determines what sound waves are needed to cancel out the "noisy" ones, and these antinoise sound waves are generated a fraction of a second later.

4. Repeat your tests with all the materials, and list them in order of how well they absorb sound. Which is the best sound insulator?

BOUNCING SOUNDS

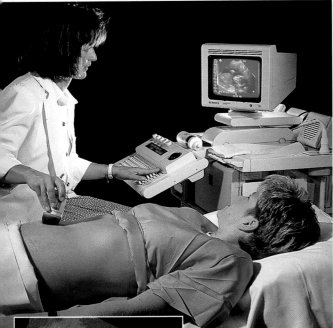

You have already learned that sound waves travel at different speeds through solids, liquids, and gases. However, sound waves do not pass very well from one substance to another. So if you shout at a brick wall, little of the sound energy will come out into the air on the other side. Instead, most of the sound waves bounce back off the wall. You will probably have noticed this when you hear an echo in a tunnel or an empty room. An echo is a reflected sound.

Echoes can be useful or they can be a nuisance. Architects use their knowledge of how sound waves are reflected when they design buildings. A noisy restaurant can be made quieter by covering the floor, walls, and ceiling with soft or bumpy materials that soak up the sounds. But the walls and ceiling of a concert hall will be built from materials that reflect the sounds of the orchestra toward the audience.

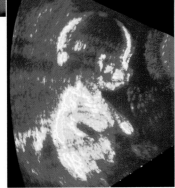

The doctor shown here is moving an ultrasound scanner across the abdomen of a pregnant woman. The inset shows the scan of the fetus inside her.

Even sound waves we cannot hear produce echoes that give us important information. Some vibrations have frequencies of several million hertz. These vibrations produce ultrasound. Ultrasound can travel through some solid objects and be reflected by others. An example is the use of ultrasound to "see" an unborn baby inside its mother's womb. Another example is sonar. This stands for "Sound Navigation and Ranging" and is used by ships to study the seafloor.

DID YOU KNOW?

Bats have poor eyesight but can hear ultrasound. Bats that eat flying insects use very high-frequency sound waves to find and chase their prey. The technique is called echolocation. Bats send out bursts of ultrasound that are reflected off any object in their path. They have large ears to collect the echo.

HEARING AROUND CORNERS

1. Arrange two cardboard tubes on a table so that they are at right angles to each other.

2. Place the clock at the end of one tube and put your ear close to the end of the other. Can you hear the tick of the clock?

3. Now cut out a square of stiff cardboard and stand it upright in modeling clay supports. Place the cardboard where the open ends of the tubes come close together.

MATERIALS

- a clock or watch with a quiet tick
- 3 to 4 similar cardboard tubes
- sound-reflecting materials, such as pieces of stiff cardboard, plastic, aluminum foil, or ceramic tiles
- modeling clay
- scissors

4. Listen again for the tick of the clock. How does the loudness of the tick compare to the first test?

5. Repeat the test with squares of the other materials. Which is the best sound reflector?

6. Next, try reflecting the sound of the ticking clock by using some of the other cardboard tubes and squares of the best sound reflecting material. How many times do you find you can reflect the sound?

A transmitter attached to the hull of a ship sends out a sonar beam that can be moved sideways or up and down to study the seafloor.

TUNING

Most sounds are a mixture of frequencies. As you walk along a street, the sound you hear is noise because it has no pattern. Sounds of only one frequency are called notes, and we call a pattern of notes music. But some combinations of notes seem like music to one person and noise to another!

Each string on a guitar is tightened until the desired pitch is reached. The guitar can be tuned to itself, to another instrument, or to a pitch set by a tuning fork.

JAM JAR BAND

MATERIALS

- 8 similar jam jars
- a set of tuning forks or a tuned musical instrument
- a rubber eraser
- some long nails
- water

Musical notes can be arranged in a pattern called a scale. The most common scale has eight notes and is called an octave. This is the scale generally used in the Western world. The notes on a piano are in octaves—you will probably have sung the notes of an octave: C, D, E, F, G, A, B, C. Other scales have fewer steps, such as the pentatonic or five-note scale of Chinese music, and some have more divisions, such as the twenty-two-note scale of classical Indian music.

Musicians who play western music frequently use tuning forks to help them adjust their instruments so that they produce the pure notes of the octave scale. These tuning forks are carefully made steel Y-shapes, each with precise measurements. When a fork is struck against a hard surface, its arms vibrate at a constant speed and produce a sound wave with only one frequency, which is stamped on the side of the fork, such as "329.6 hertz E." There are eight tuning forks in a complete set, and they produce the eight-note scale. The smallest fork makes the highest note, C, one octave higher than, and twice the frequency of, the sound produced by the largest fork. This note corresponds to "middle C" on the piano keyboard.

1. Put the 8 jars in a line. Hit the first jar with a nail and listen to the note.

2. Strike the largest tuning fork on the eraser and listen to the note. Pour a little water into the jar and hit it again with the nail. The pitch of the note is higher than before. Keep adding water until the note is the same as the one made by the tuning fork.

3. Repeat these steps with the other jars and tuning forks until you can play all the notes of the octave scale.

4. Play a simple tune with your jam jar band, either one you know, such as "Three Blind Mice," or compose one for yourself. You might need a second nail to play the tune quickly.

Keep your jam jar band safe.

DID YOU KNOW?
Some people have the ability to identify or sing a particular note without reference to any other musical note. This phenomenon is known as absolute pitch. People who can identify or sing a note with reference to another note are said to have relative pitch.

SOUND ON PAPER

Over the centuries a way of writing down music, called musical notation, developed. This is a system of written symbols that represent musical sounds. Without musical notation, musicians would have to memorize what they play. This can be very unreliable.

The standard notation of western music is called staff notation. It uses a staff of five lines with four spaces between the lines. Each line and the space between the lines represents a different pitch. Notes are drawn on a line or in a space. The length of time that each note should be played is shown by how it is drawn, and the silences, or pauses, between notes are indicated by signs called rests.

The symbols and instructions on a sheet of music, or score, give information to the musician, such as how quickly and how loudly the music should be played.

Western music is usually written on a set of five lines called a staff. The positions of the notes on the staff tell the musician what to play. Musical notation has changed little over the last century even with the arrival of computers.

DID YOU KNOW?

Musicians use a special timing device called a metronome to check that they are playing a piece of music at the right speed. It has an upright pendulum that ticks from side to side with a regular beat. The beat is altered by moving a weight up or down the pendulum, which makes the metronome beat slower or faster.

SIGNS AND SYMBOLS

1. Choose a colored shape to match each of the jars in your jam jar band. Stick the shapes onto the sides of the jars so that you know which jar to play when you read the notes.

MATERIALS
- sheets of squared paper
- stickers of 8 different colors
- the jam jar band (see pages 28–29)

2. On the left-hand side of your sheet of squared paper stick a colored shape that corresponds with the lowest note that you can play on your jars.

3. Now stick the other 7 colors onto the sheet to represent the other 7 notes in the octave. Use the squares to make the distance between each shape the same. This is your scale. Play the scale through on the jars while you look at the shapes—your notes—on the squared paper.

4. Next, try sticking shapes onto the squared paper to represent the tune you played with the jam jar band. Work through one note at a time, playing the note and then placing the shape on the paper. Don't stick them down until they all seem to be in the right places. Continue your tune on another line of the squared paper if you need to. Ask a friend to play the tune by following the notes on your sheet. Did your friend get it right?

MUSICAL PIPES

Many musical instruments have pipes. When the air inside a pipe is made to vibrate, it produces a sound. The jam jar band works like that except that striking a jar gives a different quality to the note than blowing across the top. The traditional organ is probably the best-known instrument that consists of columns of air, but other examples are found throughout the orchestra. They include wind instruments such as recorders, oboes, and clarinets and brass instruments such as trumpets and trombones.

In an organ, there are a number of hollow pipes, each one of a different length. When air is blown across the bottom end of a pipe, the air inside the pipe vibrates. The length of the pipe determines the note produced by the vibrating column of air. The shorter the pipe, the less air there is to vibrate and the higher the note. A long pipe contains a greater volume of air and vibrates more slowly, producing a lower note.

Instruments like the recorder have one pipe. The recorder comes in four sizes: the soprano, the alto, the tenor, and the bass. The smallest, called the soprano, plays the highest notes, and the bass recorder plays the lowest notes. But each size recorder can produce a range of notes itself. That is because there are holes down the front of the instrument. By opening and closing these holes with the fingers, the recorder player can lengthen or shorten the column of air vibrating inside the pipe.

PANPIPES

1. Cut 8 straws to different lengths. Blow across the top of each straw to hear the note it makes. Try to find lengths that give a wide range of notes from high to low.

MATERIALS
- 8 large drinking straws
- tape
- scissors

2. Tape the straws together so that they are level at one end. Try blowing across them to make an octave scale. Can you blow a tune on your panpipes?

CARDBOARD-TUBE RECORDER

1. Mark the places for 8 holes to be evenly spaced along the tube, leaving a 2.5-in. (6-cm) space at the end of the tube.

2. Make 8 holes in the places you have marked using the bradawl. Cut away a small piece of the tube in the middle of the 2.5-in. (6-cm) space. This will be the blowhole, where the air vibrates when the recorder is played.

3. Cut a slice off the cork to give it a flat edge and push the cork into the tube so that it fits tightly, with its flat edge facing the blow-hole. This is the mouthpiece.

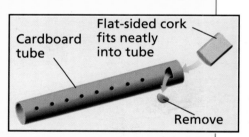

Cardboard tube

Flat-sided cork fits neatly into tube

Remove

4. Blow gently into the mouthpiece and listen to the sound. Use your fingers to cover the holes, starting with the bottom one, and find out how to play a scale.

This panpipe player is from the Andes Mountains in South America. South American panpipe music is now popular all around the world.

VALVES AND SLIDES

Brass instruments are wind instruments that are made of metal. Although they vary considerably in shape and size, from tiny trumpets to giant tubas, every brass instrument has a mouthpiece and a length of hollow tube that opens out into a bell shape. Usually the mouthpiece is cup-shaped, as in the trumpet, but it can be cone-shaped, as in the French horn. The metal tube can be an even cylinder, as it is in the trombone, or it can have a cone shape, as in the tuba.

A brass instrument is played by the musician vibrating his or her lips against the mouthpiece so that the air inside the tube vibrates. The player can change the notes made by the instrument by varying the shape of the lips. Pursing the lips makes the column of air in the tube divide into several parts. This creates a series of notes called harmonics, which have frequencies of two or three times the basic note.

Some brass instruments are fitted with valves. When a valve is pushed down, it forces the air in the pipe to travel a longer route, along an extra loop of tubing called the slide. This has the effect of making the column of air longer, so the note blown is lower. A trombone has a movable slide and there are no valves. Trombone players push the slide away from them to make the note lower and bring it toward them to make it higher.

A school band, composed of different brass instruments, playing on the steps of the Capitol in Washington, D.C.

SWANEE WHISTLE

1. Ask an adult to cut a 12-in. (30-cm) length of pipe and smooth down any cut edges. Ask them also to cut a length of dowel rod about 4 in. (10 cm) longer than the pipe.

2. Tape the mouthpiece from a plastic whistle over one end of the pipe. This will protect your lips and give a louder sound.

3. Push the dowel into the lower end of the pipe. What is the effect of raising and lowering the dowel while you are blowing into the mouthpiece? How would you describe the sound you hear? Which brass instrument does the Swanee whistle most resemble?

VALVES

The different notes played on brass instruments are produced by changing the distance the air travels down the tube. This is done either by opening and closing valves or by lengthening and shortening the tube.

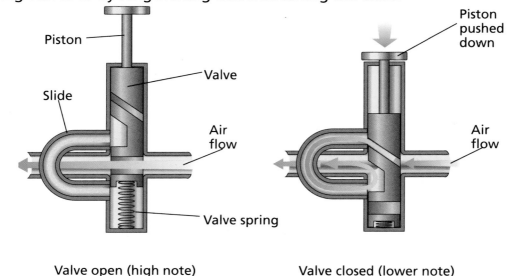

Valve open (high note)   Valve closed (lower note)

BEAT IT!

Drums are the oldest and simplest of all musical instruments. Every human culture uses drums in their music, often to create a rhythm for other instruments or singers to follow. All drums consist of a frame that contains a space filled with air. Across this frame is stretched a skin. When the skin is struck, usually with hands or with special beaters, the skin first vibrates and then the air inside the frame vibrates and amplifies the sound.

Percussion instruments produce sounds when they are struck, shaken, scraped, or crashed together. Some have a fixed note that cannot be changed, such as the triangle, cymbals, gong, or maracas. They are made from solid materials, usually metal or wood and, because the sounds they make do not involve vibrating columns of air, their sounds tend to be sharp and short-lived.

Other percussion instruments, including the xylophone and tubular bells, are tuned to a particular pitch and can play octaves. A xylophone is also made from metal or wood—often a mixture of the two—and consists of a number of bars, arranged in a similar way to the keys on a piano. Each bar is made a specific length so that it produces a sound of a certain pitch. Short bars make high notes and longer bars make lower notes.

A group of drummers and a dancer from the Ninga tribe of Burundi

TUBULAR BELLS

1. Ask an adult to cut a length of copper pipe into 8 pieces, each one .75 in. to 1 in. (2 to 3 cm) longer than the one before.

2. Lay the broom handle across the backs of two chairs.

3. Cut 8 similar pieces of string and tie the first to the broom handle. Take the shortest tube and use tape to attach the tube to the piece of string. Repeat this for the other tubes, trying to get them to hang straight and at the same height.

4. Strike the tubes gently with a long nail to make them ring. Try to play a scale and a tune on your tubular bells.

STRING SOUNDS

Stringed instruments such as the violin and the guitar make their sounds when strings are bowed or plucked, or struck, as in the case of keyboard instruments such as the piano.

A vibrating string makes very little sound on its own. To make the sound louder, most stringed instruments have hollow bodies known as the sound box. The sound box, or resonator, picks up the vibrations made by the strings and amplifies the sound.

The pattern of sound waves produced by a stringed instrument depends on three things: the length of the string, how tight it is, and what the string is made of. You may have seen violinists or guitar players use their fingers to hold down the strings on their instruments at different places. This has the effect of shortening the strings and changing the note that you hear. A long string gives a low note; a short string gives a higher one.

At the end of the soundboard on a stringed instrument there are special pegs called tuning pegs (or tuning machines on a guitar). There is a peg attached to each string, and the player turns the pegs to change the tightness, or tension, on the string. The instrument is correctly tuned when the tension on each string produces the desired note.

A string quartet comprises four string instruments, usually two violins, a viola, and a cello. The leader of the quartet is known as the first violinist.

BOX GUITARS

1. Cut three or four identical wedge-shaped pieces of thick cardboard the same width as your small shoebox. Glue them together to make the bridge of the guitar.

MATERIALS

- empty boxes of different sizes, such as matchboxes and shoeboxes
- assorted elastic bands or elastic cord
- thick cardboard
- glue
- scissors

2. Cut out a circle near one end of your shoebox. This will let the sound out of the resonator.

3. Stretch four or five elastic bands along the length of the shoebox so that they fit over the bridge, which should be placed on the other side of the hole. You can now play your shoebox guitar.

4. Repeat the process to build a guitar from a larger shoebox. You will need to construct a bigger bridge, and you should be able to add more strings. On a large shoebox, you may need to use knotted lengths of elastic cord instead of elastic bands. How does the sound compare with the smaller box guitar?

STORING SOUNDS

For many years, people have been used to buying music on vinyl, a type of plastic. The sound on a vinyl record is stored as a wiggly groove, a kind of copy of the sound wave that made it. A sharp stylus sits in the groove as the record turns. As the stylus bounces from side to side, its vibrations are turned into small electrical signals by wire coils that vibrate near a magnet. These signals are sent to an amplifier where they are made larger, before being passed on to loudspeakers, which change the signals back into sound waves.

Because people wanted to make their own recordings, a different form of recording was needed. This led to the development of magnetic recording tapes. Recording tape is a long strip of plastic coated with magnetic particles. On a tape recorder the tape moves past a magnet that is receiving an electrical signal from a microphone. Changes in the electrical signal produce a similar pattern of changes in the magnetic field, and this pattern is copied onto the magnetic particles of the tape to make the recording.

There are two types of sound recording: analog and digital. Analog recordings store the patterns of sound waves as grooves on vinyl records or patterns of magnetic particles on cassette tapes.

RECORDING SOUNDS

1. Practice recording voices in a room using the microphone. What is the effect of changing the recording level? How are the recordings different when you hold the microphone close to or away from the speaker?

2. Record the same voices in a large open space. Do you have to change the recording level to get good recordings? How good is the microphone at picking up sounds in the open? How good is the microphone at picking up sounds at longer distances?

MATERIALS

- a portable cassette tape recorder (preferably with recording level controls)
- a separate microphone on a lead
- headphones
- a large umbrella
- tape
- a cassette tape
- scissors

Digital recordings change the sound signal into numbers that represent the sound waves and then store these numbers as pits on a compact disc. A beam of laser light is shined onto the disc. If it hits a pit, it bounces away and is not used. If it bounces off a flat area, it is electronically sensed as a pulse of light. The pulses are then changed into electrical signals to be amplified and converted back into sounds. Compact discs give a higher quality sound reproduction than vinyl records or cassette tapes.

3. Open the umbrella and tape the microphone to the handle so it is pointing away from the handle. You have now made what is called a parabolic reflector. Sound waves bounce off the underside of the umbrella and are collected by the microphone.

4. Repeat your outdoor recordings and see how far away you can go and still make good recordings of voices.

DID YOU KNOW?

More than a century ago, in 1877, Thomas Edison invented the first machine that recorded sound. He called it a phonograph, or "sound-writer." Edison shouted down a short cone to make a needle vibrate against a sheet of tinfoil wrapped around a cylinder, which he turned as he spoke. The vibrating needle scratched a groove in the foil, which Edison could then play by putting the needle back to the start of the groove and listening at the end of a longer cone as he turned the cylinder.

CALL ME

Sounds do not usually travel very far. That is because the energy in a sound wave is absorbed by the air. To send a message farther, you need to change the sound signal into an electrical one. The device that carries out this change is a microphone. You also need a device for changing electrical energy back into sound. Speakers do that.

Both microphones and speakers are important parts of any device that helps send sound messages across long distances.

High-quality microphones contain a thin plate, or diaphragm, that vibrates when someone speaks into the microphone. A coil of thin wire is attached to the diaphragm and

moves up and down with it. When the coil vibrates, it moves between the north and south poles of a magnet, and this produces an electrical signal in the coil. In a telephone, the signal then travels along copper wires to a loudspeaker, which is in the earpiece of the other telephone.

Although speakers look very different from microphones, they share many of the same parts. Both have a diaphragm, a moving coil of wire, and a magnet. When the electrical signal arrives from the microphone, it passes through the coil and creates a changing magnetic field. This reacts with the magnet, so that the coil is sometimes attracted to it and sometimes repelled by it. The coil vibrates in and out very quickly and, because the diaphragm is attached to the coil, it moves as well. This creates vibrations in the air around the speaker, which we hear as sounds.

A mobile phone contains a transmitter as well as a mouthpiece and a receiver. The transmitter changes the sound waves into radio waves, so that they can be sent through the air instead of along metal wires.

A woman using a videophone, a modern telecommunications machine that enables you to see a picture of the person you are talking to.

CROSS SECTION OF PHONE HANDSET

Inside the microphone of many phones there is a thin space filled with grains of carbon. When you speak, the sound waves push a diaphragm against the carbon grains and squeeze them closer together. This changes the pattern of an electrical current flowing through them. This new pattern becomes the signal that travels down the phone line.

Diaphragm

Receiver

Electromagnet

Diaphragm

Carbon particles

Transmitter

MAKE A TELEPHONE

MATERIALS

- 30 to 60 ft. (10 to 20 m) of insulated electrical wire
- a roll of thin copper wire
- 2 yogurt containers or strong plastic cups
- 2 cylinder magnets from a model-making shop
- thin paper
- cardboard
- strong glue
- tape
- scissors

1. First make a cardboard tube to fit snugly around the magnet. Cut a strip of cardboard .75 in. to 1 in. (2 to 3 cm) wider than the length of the magnet. Roll the strip around the magnet and glue the tube along the long edge.

2. Cut two cardboard circles and make a hole in each one large enough for them to fit like collars over the ends of the tube. Snip the ends of the tube to make six small flaps. Glue the flaps to the collars to make a reel.

3. Wind 50 to 60 turns of thin copper wire around the reel, and cut it to leave the two ends clearly visible. You have now made a wire coil.

4. Now make a support for the reel. This will hold it securely inside the cup. Cut a circle of cardboard slightly larger than the open end of the plastic cup and place the reel at the center. Cut down to the reel from the edge of the cardboard to make 6 or 8 V-shapes, as shown. Glue one end of the reel to the center of the support.

5. Make a hole in the bottom of the plastic cup and pass through two strands of the insulated wire. Connect the ends of the insulated wires to the free ends of the copper coil.

6. Cut a thin paper diaphragm the same size as the supports for the reel. Make about 20 cuts around the edge of the paper circle to give a number of small flaps. Bend the flaps up.

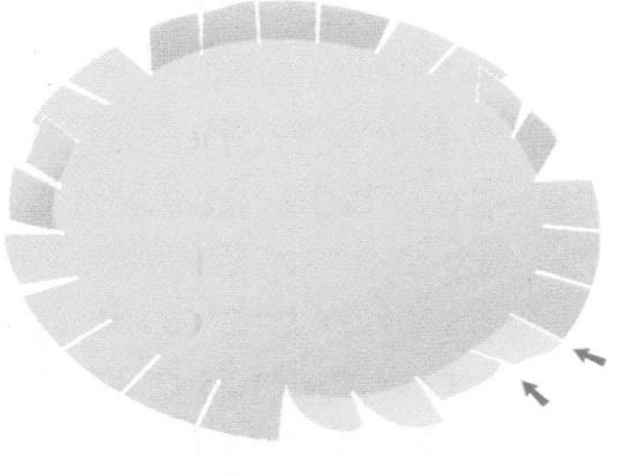

6

7. Cut a circle of cardboard the same size as the collars on the reel, and glue it to the center of the diaphragm. Glue the magnet to this circle.

7

8. Dab glue on the "arms" of the reel support and push it down into the plastic cup so that the top of the reel is .75 in. to 1 in. (2 to 3 cm) below the rim of the pot. Be careful that the wires do not come apart as you do this. Let the glue dry.

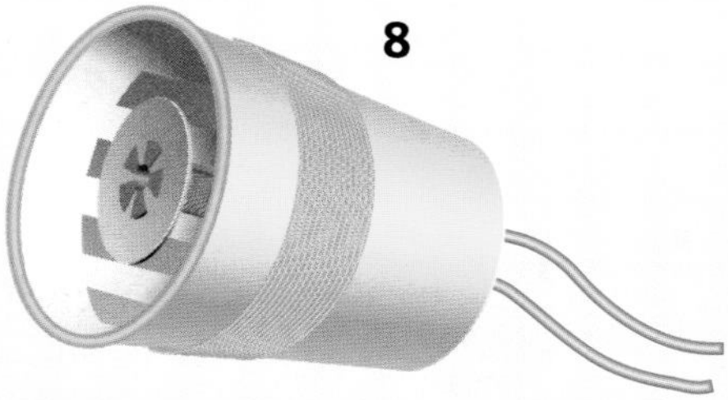

8

9. Glue the flaps of the diaphragm inside the rim of the cup so that the magnet hangs down into the reel. Let the glue dry.

10. Repeat steps 1–9 with the second plastic cup, joining the coil to the other ends of the insulated wires.

9

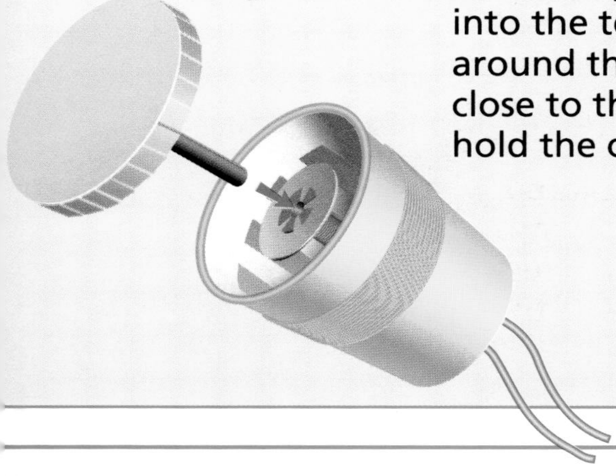

11. Stretch out the insulated wires between you and a friend. To talk into the telephone, cup your hands around the pot and speak clearly close to the diaphragm. To listen, hold the cup close to your ear.

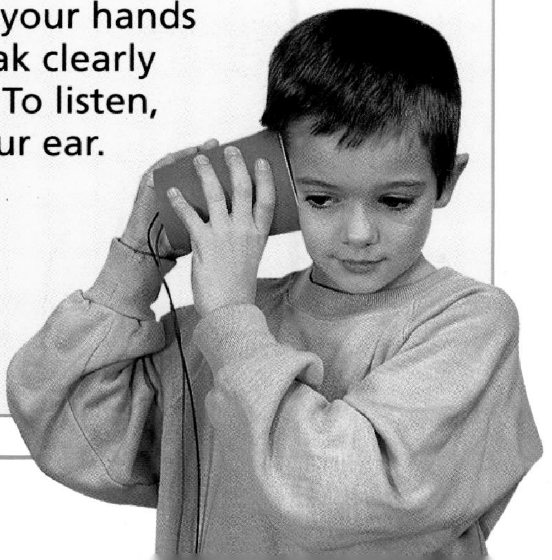

GLOSSARY

Amplify To make sounds louder.

Amplitude The "height" of a sound wave. The larger the amplitude of a sound wave, the louder it is.

Auditory nerve The nerve that carries electrical signals from the cochlea to the brain.

Bridge A piece of wood or metal that connects the strings of a stringed instrument to the soundboard.

Cochlea A spiral-shaped bony tube inside the ear. It is filled with liquid and lined with tiny hairs that change vibrations in the liquid into electrical signals that go to the brain.

Decibel (dB) A measurement of loudness. The decibel scale starts at 0, which is silence. It has no maximum number, but sounds above 120 decibels are painful to hear.

Eardrum A membrane of skin inside the ear that vibrates when struck by sound waves.

Frequency The number of sound waves per second. It is measured in hertz (Hz), named after the German physicist, Heinrich Hertz.

Larynx The space at the top of the windpipe that contains the vocal cords.

Loudspeaker A device that changes electrical signals into sound waves.

Microphone A device that converts sound waves into electrical signals.

Noise A mixture of sound waves with no regular wave pattern; an unwanted sound.

Note A sound played at a particular frequency, or pitch. It is also a written symbol for a sound in musical notation.

Percussion instruments Musical instruments that are played by being struck, shaken, scraped, or crashed together. Examples are drums, maracas, and tubular bells.

Pitch How high or low a note is. Sound waves with a high pitch are close together.

Resonator An air-filled space inside an instrument that makes the sounds louder.

Soundboard The part of a stringed instrument that is connected to the strings by the bridge. When the strings are plucked, the resonator vibrates.

Staff A set of five lines, separated by four spaces, on which musical notes are written.

Tuning fork A metal instrument that vibrates at one pitch. It is used to tune musical instruments.

Vacuum A completely empty space where there are no air particles. Outer space is a vacuum.

Wavelength The distance between one crest of a sound wave and the next. Sound waves with a short wavelength have a high frequency, and sounds with a long wavelength have a low frequency.

FURTHER INFORMATION

BOOKS

Catherall, Ed. *Exploring Sound.* Exploring Science. Austin, TX: Raintree Steck-Vaughn, 1990.

Darling, David. *Sounds Interesting: The Science of Acoustics.* Experiments! Parsippany, NJ: Silver Burdett Press, 1991.

Morgan, Sally & Morgan, Adrian. *Using Sound.* Designs in Science. New York: Facts on File, 1994.

CD-ROMS

Exploring Science – Light and Sound Austin, TX: Raintree Steck-Vaughn, 1997.

ANSWERS TO QUESTIONS

Answers to questions posed in the projects.

Pages 6–7 Louder sounds make the spot move a greater distance from side to side. A higher note makes the spot vibrate faster.

Pages 8–9 When you shake your hand faster, you produce waves of greater frequency. When you shake your hand farther from side to side or up and down, you increase the amplitude, so the size of the waves becomes greater. To make waves of higher frequency in a Slinky®, you will need to push the Slinky® faster. To make waves of greater amplitude, you will need to push harder.

Pages 12–13 You should be able to observe that the light signal takes less time than the sound signal to pass around the triangle. If the experimenters are 650 ft. (200 m) apart, the sound signal will take about two seconds plus reaction times, so five seconds in all. The light signal is almost instantaneous, so the observer is measuring reaction times only, about three seconds in all.

Pages 14–15 Bigger tubes make a lower note since a greater volume of air is vibrating. The faster you twirl the tube, the easier it is to notice the Doppler effect. You will hear a higher note as the tube comes toward your ears, and a lower note as it moves away from you.

Pages 16–17 Depending on the accent you are trying to imitate, you will have to shape your lips in a certain way and change the way you say the sounds of groups of letters. You may even have to pinch your nose a little to make the air vibrate with a different note from your usual voice.

Pages 18–19 Covering one ear with soundproofing material will reduce the accuracy with which you can pinpoint sounds. Two ears are needed if the direction of a source of sound is to be judged accurately.

Pages 24–25 Soft materials with uneven surfaces such as carpet tiles or felt are the best insulators because the sound waves break up. Hard, shiny surfaces are good reflectors of sound waves.

Pages 34–35 Pushing the dowel into the Swanee whistle reduces the volume of air vibrating in the tube and produces a higher note. The whistle works in much the same way as the trombone.

Pages 38–39 A larger box guitar will generally produce lower notes than those produced by a smaller box because the volume of air vibrating is greater. However, this assumes that the tension in the strings is the same.

INDEX